THE GODS I WORSHIP

THE GODS I WORSHIP

Z. E. MANLEY

Z&A PRESS

Eden, Utah

© 2017 Zena E. Manley

THE GODS I WORSHIP

All rights reserved. No part of this book may be reproduced in any form or by any means without permission, in writing, from the publisher, Z to A Press, at contact@ztoapress.com or P.O. Box 343, Eden, Utah 84310.

This work is not an official publication of The Church of Jesus Christ of Latter-day Saints ("Church"). The views expressed herein are the responsibility of the authors and do not necessarily represent the position of the Church or of Z to A Press.

Visit us at ztoapress.com

Cover designed by Zena E. Manley
"Beautiful Eclipse" created by Freepik

ISBN: 978-0-578-19748-7

to the
WORKINGTON BRANCH
for giving me a home
on the other side of the world

and SISTERS N. DAVIES & H. THOMPSON
for the opportunity to
be a member missionary in Cumbria

Thank you.

Contents

Preface xii
The Gods' Purpose for Mortality 1
The Eternal Father 26
Jesus The Christ 51
The Holy Ghost 80
The Children of God 103
Notes 119

DISCLAIMER

I do not represent The Church of Jesus Christ of Latter-day Saints. Consequently, if there are any discrepancies between what is found in this book and the official doctrines of the Church, the fault is mine.

Acknowledgements

This book only came about because my mom requested a summary of the gospel that she could use to help her in her calling as a missionary. Therefore, as always, I am in your debt, Mom.

Naturally, my thanks go to both my parents, who were the first to read this manuscript, correct my spelling, and ask the most piercing of questions. You have always been the readers I wanted most to impress. Thank you for sticking with the pages all these years.

My profound gratitude to my editor, Kathy Carter. Without her talent, intelligence, thoughtfulness, and technical skills, this book would still be an unintelligible manuscript. I deeply appreciate her precision, dedication, and encouragements.

To my friends, who gave their valuable time to proofread the grammar, and more importantly, debated and discussed the doctrine with me, you deserve far more recognition than you get.

Additionally, I am perpetually beholden to all the teachers who have given their time, talents, and efforts in spoon-feeding me the gospel throughout my life. Your callings as teachers and friends may go universally unheralded, but they are not wasted, and they will never be forgotten by me.

Lastly, and although it seems trite to thank the divine Gods, I know I could not have written this without Their inspiration, let alone exist to attempt it. Never have two words fallen shorter in scope and yet they are all I have: THANK YOU.

Preface

I am a Christian. I am a member of The Church of Jesus Christ of Latter-day Saints, otherwise known as a Mormon, a Latter-Day Saint, or LDS. I "talk of Christ, [I] rejoice in Christ, [I] preach of Christ…and [I] write…that our children may know to what source they may look for a remission of their sins." (2 Nephi 25:26).

I am not an expert of theology, I hold no prestigious doctorates, I have won no awards for writing, I hold no distinctive positions of power, and I speak with no authority from my church.

What I am is a person of faith with a personal testimony that the words I write in this book are true. I have not seen a vision, nor have I heard the voices of angels; however, the Spirit of God has whispered to my soul truths I cannot deny. I know, from the millions of prayers I have offered and the years I have spent reading the scriptures, that the invisible divine workings of God are tangible, practical, and accessible. The gospel of Jesus Christ is as alive and as dynamically a part of our daily lives as the Gods who created it.

As such, I give you all the accreditation I can, my name and my faith, as my witness to you that Jesus Christ, the Son of the Eternal Father, does in fact redeem us of our sins, saves us from death, and brings us back to the glories of heaven from which we came, if we choose to let Him do so.

The title of this book, *The Gods I Worship*, was very carefully chosen, as it immediately establishes the chief difference found in my faith in contrast to the other sects of Christianity. It is the main point of doctrine that needs defining, as all other doctrine stems from this foundation of who and what God is.

God the Eternal Father, Jesus Christ, and the Holy Ghost are three distinct gods. While They work in perfect harmony, for a singular purpose, They are individual beings, with unique titles and responsibilities in the overall perfecting of the human race. The Father, the Son, and the Holy Ghost are the Gods I worship.

This definition of God and the Godhead may seem unnecessary to a member of the Mormon faith as it will appear automatic to them. In contrast, this same definition may seem blasphemous to members of other Christian sects as it is in such sharp contrast to their own understanding of the nature of God.

It was here, in this immediate difference in definition, vocabulary, and assumed contrasting knowledge that I grew up in. Both of my parents are converts to the Mormon faith. Most of my extended family are, or were, Catholic.

The rest are agnostic or atheist. Consequently, I was raised in a home where the doctrine of Jesus Christ was taught with the fundamental understanding that the words of the Lord needed detailed defining.

After all, to assume that all faiths, Christian or otherwise, meant the same thing when they used the same words was a mistake. Without taking the time to explain the terminology of their faith, I watched, and participated in many conversations where both sides thought they had swayed the other to their way of believing, when in fact neither had understood what the other had said. This I have found to be universally true and not just a unique dynamic of my family.

For instance, the word "god" can be utterly meaningless, simply a mark of punctuation to indicate happiness, or conversely, a curse of anger. In both circumstances, a holy being is unlikely associated with the word.

To those who have faith, the word "God" can mean a wide variety of deities associated with infinite doctrines and world beliefs. Within the wide net of Christianity, the word "God" comes with a hotly contested definition. Is God one person or three? Is God a he, a she, or an it? Does God exist at all or is he merely symbolic, a psychological manifestation of comfort or control, a cultural crutch, or a manipulative devise of the government?

As a member of The Church of Jesus Christ of Latter-day Saints, I grew up with a precise definition of who and what God is. Thanks to my family dynamic, I also grew up knowing that our particular definition of God, specifically that there are three separate Gods in the Godhead, made me different than other Christians.

However, I'm sure that there are many Mormons that do not realize how radically different that understanding of God is from other faiths. Indeed, as a member of any church, it is easy to forget that our vocabulary is so different from one another that it becomes almost impossible for the listener to understand the message we are trying to share if we do not take the time to define the words we use.

Consequently, when my mom asked me to write a summary of the gospel for use as a missionary tool, I immediately decided to write it from the perspective of the investigator as opposed to the teacher. The result of that decision is the book that follows.

The Gods I Worship is not meant to be a comprehensive examination and explanation of Mormon theology; rather, this book is written as a summary of doctrinal concepts, each point leading to the next in a simplified fashion that should lend itself to teaching and personal study.

The introductory chapter, *The God's Purpose for Mortality*, is a broad overview of life, including the pre-mortal, mortal, and post-mortal phases of the human lifespan. The next three chapters, *The Eternal Father, Jesus the Christ, and the Holy Ghost*, focus on the Gods as individuals and how the three Gods work as one Godhead in aiding mankind with our immortality and eternal life.

The concluding chapter, *The Children of God*, examines the role we all play in our own salvation as well as our responsibility in sharing the message that we have received from the Gods to the rest of the human race.

Finally, while there are scripture references throughout this text, I found it impossible to cite the root of every thought of theology found herein without listing the entirety of the scriptures. Due to the need for brevity in a work such as this, I have listed the main scriptural citations I used in the reference chapter entitled *Notes*.

Naturally for a truly in-depth study of the gospel, I suggest that the reader turn to the unfiltered word of God found throughout the entirety of the scriptures and ask the Spirit to teach them what I can in nowise adequately summarize here.

My hope is that *The Gods I Worship* can give the Mormon reader the courage to teach the fundamentals of the gospel of Jesus Christ (with particular focus on the doctrines of the Godhead), the purpose of life, the function of the priesthood, the necessity of temple covenants, and the nature of eternity to someone who knows none of the LDS vocabulary the teacher may take for granted.

Additionally, I hope this book sparks an interest in any readers curious in the foreign doctrines associated with Mormonism and I highly recommend that they pursue their interest in the restored gospel of Jesus Christ by contacting the local Mormon missionaries.

While I have done my best to answer any questions I can foresee coming up in a general discussion, it is the missionaries who will be able to answer questions with the precise aid of the Holy Ghost. Mormon missionaries can be contacted by going to: www.mormon.org.

Lastly, whomever you, dear reader, might be, I reiterate my invitation to you to read the LDS canonized scriptures: the *Holy Bible*, the *Book of Mormon*, the *Doctrine and Covenants*, and the *Pearl of Great Price*.

In addition, I implore you to study the words of the living prophets of The Church of Jesus Christ of Latter-day Saints. Every six months a General Conference is held where these prophets, apostles, and general auxiliary leaders of the Church meet, speak, advise, teach, and testify of Christ and His salvation. Their words can be found by visiting: www.lds.org.

Listen to the ancient and modern prophets. They listen to the Gods I worship.

The Gods' Purpose for Mortality

I worship God, the Eternal Father, and His Son, Jesus Christ, and the Holy Ghost (Articles of Faith 1:1). They are three individual Gods. The Father, called Elohim, and the Son, called Jehovah or Jesus Christ, have resurrected bodies of flesh and bone. The Holy Ghost has a spirit body (Doctrine & Covenants 130:22-23). While separate in Their physical, literal forms, They are united in a singular divine purpose, thus the three are often referred to as one. In this unity, They are called the Godhead.

The Father, the Son, and the Holy Ghost are the Gods I worship. They are my family. This mortal life is a time set apart for us to come to know Them by proving ourselves to

THE GODS' PURPOSE FOR MORTALITY

Them through obedience and sacrifice in all things.

The very nature of mortality makes this task complicated in that They deliberately prevent us from remembering Them, despite our having lived in Their presence for eons before this mortal life. This purposeful amnesia is called the veil. The veil was placed upon our memories in order that we might pass through this mortal life in a state of faith. The veil is also the natural recourse of the fall of Adam and Eve.

When Adam and Eve partook of the fruit in the Garden of Eden, and thereby disobeyed the Gods, they committed a transgression that, as forewarned, instituted death into the world. We call this the Fall of Adam and Eve or simply the Fall. The resulting death of the Fall came in two forms: spiritual death and physical death—sometimes interchangeably called the first and second deaths.

It is important to note that this was the plan from the beginning. The Gods were not thwarted by the manipulative schemes of Satan presented to Adam and Eve in the Garden. We are not muddling through Plan B. We, the descendants of Adam and Eve, draw breath upon this planet because they chose to risk the uncertainties of mortality for the certainties of eternity.

Eve was the first to partake of the fruit of "the tree of the knowledge of good and evil" in order to gain the requisite knowledge to progress (Moses 3:17). Adam, her husband, partook of the fruit second so that he could remain with her and father the human race. Their sacrifices were necessary, as were the results of their transgression. Spiritual death and physical death give purpose to mortality.

Spiritual death is the separation between God the Eternal Father and ourselves. Physical death is the separation between our spirits and our bodies. All descendants of Adam and Eve are born with these inherent divisions. However, we are also born into a world in which the Atonement of Jesus Christ has broken the "bands of death" in both its forms (Mosiah 16:7–8).

Adam and Eve were taught this in the Garden. It was in the height of their pain, knowing that they were to be separated from the physical presence of God, that God explained that His Son would make it possible for them to return. This plan, succinctly called the Atonement of Jesus Christ, overcomes spiritual death through repentance and forgiveness and overcomes physical death by resurrection. Mortal life began with their joy in the redemptive powers of Christ and their love for the Father who had prepared all things from the beginning.

Life existed long before we were formed here. Life before birth is often called the pre-mortal life to help distinguish it from this one; but in reality, life is simply life. We have lived for a very long time and we will continue to live forever. There is no end. There was life before the veil. There will be life after the grave. The Atonement allows for the post-mortal life to be magnificent beyond the understandings of mortality.

That is the plan of God. It is the plan that was presented to us before we crossed through the veil to this mortal proving ground. We were people with opinions and traits as varied and layered in the first estate as we are today. The first estate is the proper name for what we also call the pre-mortal life (Jude 1:6). We had thoughts, personalities, attributes, and faults. Even then, we made choices. Standing in the presence of the Gods, we, like Adam and Eve in the Garden, were independent in our thoughts. We chose as we reasoned.

Naturally, as in any household, some children were more faithful in their obedience than others. And as is true in any kingdom,

THE GODS' PURPOSE FOR MORTALITY

there were factions—some loyal, others treacherous.

In the heavenly kingdom of our Father, it appears that the vast majority of His children were faithful, loyal, and longing to do the best they could. However, there were dissenters. The chief among these traitors was Lucifer, now called Satan or the devil.

Lucifer's greatest treachery occurred at a time when our Father had gathered us in a great council to present His plan. Our Father told us that at last the time had arrived when we would come to mortality, receive a physical body, and be tested and "proven in all things" (Abraham 3:25). We, the faithful and loyal, rejoiced at the news. It was what we had been prepared for, what we had longed for. The Father presented His Son, Jehovah, the Firstborn, as the means by which we would return to our Father. It was understood that we would not pass through this mortal sojourn with perfect obedience, and it was for this cause that Jehovah, in His perfection, would redeem us from our imperfection.

Lucifer, perhaps sensing that his rebellious schemes were running out of time, stepped forth and presented his own lesser plan. His plan was designed to deny us the glories that our Father had in mind. Furthermore, at the heart of Lucifer's plan lay his attempt to dethrone God and place himself in the Father's stead. It was Lucifer's attempt at a coup d'état.

This treacherous event is called the War in Heaven. The children of Elohim, known as the host of heaven, became divided into groups or parts. A third part of that host, often called the one-third, followed Lucifer in his attack against Elohim. We do not know how many legions fought under that dark standard of treason; what we do know is that they lost.

Michael, the archangel, who would soon be called Adam, led the rest of the children of God against this rebellion. Lucifer and his followers were cast out. The followers of Satan failed in their first estate.

We did not fail in our first estate. Every mortal has the certain knowledge that in the day of rebellion, we stood with God. Whatever else our standing may have been—however obedient or partially involved we had been up to that point in our lives—when it truly mattered, we stepped up, held our ground, and chose to follow God. We kept our first estate.

This valiant decision, made in a day we cannot remember, earned us an eternal reward. Every single member of the human race is guaranteed this reward. Everyone who chose to stand with God that day has been or will be born into this mortal life and be given a physical body. Whether or not we keep this second estate, called mortality, by the choices we make to follow or fight God, we will not be denied our bodies.

The resurrection is the gift of our reward for our faithfulness in the first estate. Physical death is a necessary requirement of this life. We will all die; our spirits will separate from our bodies. This is what causes mortal death. However, in time and in order, we will all be resurrected. Our spirits will be reunited with a perfected form of this mortal flesh, never again to be separated. This resurrected state is called immortality.

Jesus Christ was the first to be resurrected. He held the keys of death. He commanded His spirit out of His body on the cross. No mortal man killed Him. He alone sent His spirit back into heaven, and when the sign of the three days had been shown, He forever broke the bands of death by returning His spirit to His then immortal body. The promised resurrection was brought into the world for all mankind. After Jesus's resurrection, many of the faithful saints were resurrected as well. This began the Morning of the First Resurrection.

The Morning of the First Resurrection is not the length of a morning. It is an era of time that began with Christ's resurrection and will continue until it has been declared at an end. The saints of God—including us, if we live as we have been commanded—will all be resurrected within this time period. Following this initial class of graduates, there will be other distinct time periods of resurrection, until ultimately, all who ever received a body of flesh will be resurrected. Immortality is the reward of the first estate.

The reward of the second estate is forgiveness, which we call eternal life. Just as immortality is guaranteed to all who kept their first estate through obedience to God's plan, eternal life is a guarantee to all who keep this second one by making the same choice of obedience. We do this by continuing to stand against Satan by living our lives under the banner of our Father in the ongoing civil war of our family.

Due to their treachery, Satan and his host of rebels will never have physical bodies. They have forfeited their right to progression. They are locked in a damnation of their own choosing. And while they rage on, they have already lost. They were never going to win this war, yet they fought it in the royal courts of our Father, and they still fight it now in the trenches of mortality. While there is no victory for them in which they win back what should have been theirs, even immortality and eternal life, they have settled on a lesser trophy, our destruction. They are not a passive enemy. Yet we have guardians to protect us, and they are not passive either.

While the veil necessarily blinds us from the workings of the other side, more accurately called the Godhead, we are not hidden from Them. They know our every concern, burden, fear, and loss, and conversely, our every joy, hope, faith, and triumph. The Gods have not left us alone, nor have Their followers. We are surrounded by angels in quantities that vastly outnumber the ranks of our enemies. They are there to counteract the would-be destroying tide of the traitors in our midst. Chief amongst those holy protectors is the Holy Ghost.

The Holy Ghost is there for all mankind. He inspires greatness, grants clarity, brings understanding, and delivers strength to all who would give Him ear. He is the pilot light of our souls. Without Him there could be no flame of faith. This divine spark is given to all. We were born with it. It is part of our inheritance from Adam and Eve—an eternal calling card from our first parents to look to the Gods and live. The Holy Ghost, also called the Spirit, is our great teacher. He is forever stirring up our hearts in remembrance of the Father and the Son.

The Holy Ghost exists for all the human race. All men, women, and children can feel the inspiring influence of the Holy Ghost in their lives at critical moments whether or not they know anything of Him or the Godhead.

However, the Holy Ghost can be more than a sporadic presence in our lives.

The Father has given mankind the priesthood to perform sacred ordinances which lead to the salvation of His children. The priesthood is the authority and power to act in God's name. Ordinances are official rites and ceremonies such as the blessing of the sacramental bread and water, baptism, and the confirmation of the Holy Ghost for the Gift of the Holy Ghost. Once we pass through the gates of baptism and receive the Gift of the Holy Ghost through these priesthood ordinances, we have the opportunity to have the Holy Ghost in our lives perpetually, not just sporadically.

This gift can be utilized when we demonstrate our desire to use it. We must remember Christ, we must follow Him, we must be willing to wear His name, and then we are promised that the Holy Ghost will be our personal, constant companion (Moroni 4:3). To wear the name of Christ means that we are living our lives in such a way that one glance at us can tell the most casual of observers that we believe and follow the teachings of Christ. It is to be the proverbial city on the hill that cannot be hid (Matthew 5:14). When we strive to live our lives to bring others to Christ, the Holy Ghost becomes our natural constant companion.

The Godhead works in perfect order in our mortal lives. The Holy Ghost teaches and reminds us of Jesus Christ. Jesus Christ breaks the bands of death and restores us through resurrection and repentance unto Elohim, the Eternal Father. And because the Eternal Father's purpose is to bring to pass our immortality and eternal life, He provided His Son to be our Savior, and He sends forth the Holy Ghost to inspire us. Each God works in harmony with the other for our good.

Is it any wonder that we rejoiced when we first heard this plan? These are not some distant, petty, cruel gods sitting upon Mount Olympus, toying with man for their amusements and jealousies. The Godhead is a family—a father and two sons doing all they can to save the rest of Their family and bring them home as They promised from the beginning. They are devoted to the eternal wellbeing of the entire human race.

This mortal life was designed by Them for our good. However, it was not fashioned to be a vacation. Mortal life is a proving ground—one designed to test us in all things.

Because the Gods understand that such a test would break us all, compassion, forgiveness, mercy, and love are integral to the laws of justice that govern us in this second estate. Knowing that a veiled intuition would not be enough to guide us through the complexities of this test, the Gods gave us prophets. Prophets are men with the priesthood who receive, through inspiration and direct communication from the Gods, all the requisite knowledge needed to teach us so that we can be obedient in this estate. Beginning in the days of Adam and Eve and continuing throughout time unto our present day, prophets have made faith and obedience possible, generation after generation.

Throughout recorded human history there have been seven great time periods in which this knowledge of the purposes of the Gods has been made known to mankind. These time periods are called dispensations. Each dispensation is headed by a prophet of restoration. These prophets have brought the truth to an age of people who had lost a portion of that truth through disobedience toward the previously revealed knowledge of God. This truth is called the gospel. While singular in its message, the gospel is made up of many parts, called doctrines and principles. The established hierarchy, designed to protect the gospel and disperse it to as many people as possible, is the organized church of Christ, named in this dispensation as The Church of Jesus Christ of Latter-day Saints (Doctrine and Covenants 115:3-4).

The head of the first dispensation was, fittingly, Adam. Adam was a righteous man, and his wife, Eve, was a righteous woman. Although they transgressed a law by partaking of the forbidden fruit—and the promised consequences of death, including being driven from the Garden of Eden into a lesser earth filled with thorns and trials, caused by reason of that transgression—Adam and Eve were not deemed evil, disowned, or forgotten by the Gods. Adam and Eve were loved by the Gods and loved Them in turn with all their might, mind, and strength.

Beautifully, because Adam and Eve were the first to partake of disobedience in this second estate, they were also the first to be redeemed by the Atonement of Christ. Consequently, while Jesus Christ is our example of perfection and our great teacher and guide to salvation, Adam and Eve are our examples of mortality. We have been commanded to look to them for a pattern of how to live our lives. We will all transgress and sin, and like our first parents, we can all overcome those failings through the Atonement of Jesus Christ, rejoice in the knowledge of our redemption, and teach it to our children.

It is our lot in life to come to know the Gods as our first parents did. Although imperfect, we can be forgiven and be restored to all that is meant to be ours. Mortality is the means by which we are refined into immortality and eternal life. We have the testimonies of Adam and Eve. They knew. Theirs was not a vague faith; it was a certain knowledge.

Our first parents had seen the Gods face to face. They had walked with Them, spoken with Them, and were taught by Them before the Fall. Once they were driven from the Garden in order that they might start mortality for all of us, they continued to receive revelation, allowing Adam to start the first dispensation of the gospel. Faith in the prophets' knowledge became the pattern of spiritual education in this mortal life.

In time, although Adam and Eve taught their children that the Gods existed, that They had purpose and power, and it was toward Them that they were to strive for salvation, their children stopped listening. This too is a pattern of mortality. It is for this reason of self-inflicted deafness that there have been seven major dispensations of restoration. Each time the gospel has been restored upon the earth, governed by a singular prophet, often called the head of a dispensation.

While the gospel has been taught to millions throughout history in many far-flung corners of the earth, by hundreds if not thousands of prophets, these constant teachings are not identified as one of the major dispensations, although they are equally important to the preaching and leading of mankind back unto the Gods. Therefore, there are only seven recognized, overarching dispensations.

The first dispensation, as previously stated, was overseen by Adam. The second dispensation was led by Enoch, the great founder of the city of Enoch often called the city of Zion. The people of Enoch's city were so exceedingly righteous that they were translated and taken from this earth. To be translated means that a person is changed from a normal state of mortality into one where they do not experience physical pain and are not subject to death. A translated being remains in this state of changed mortality until the time of the resurrection when they will become immortal.

After Enoch and his people were translated the third dispensation began and was governed by Noah. The prophet of the fourth dispensation was Abraham; of the fifth, Moses.

The sixth dispensation came at the prophesied "meridian of time" and was governed by Jesus Christ himself (Moses 7:46). And lastly, the seventh and promised final dispensation, called the Dispensation of the Fullness of Times, was overseen by the prophet Joseph Smith, Jr.

In this current era, the Dispensation of the Fullness of Times, we have been promised that the gospel will not be lost due to the disobedience of mankind. It will remain intact, with the powers of the priesthood governing it until the day that Jesus Christ returns to the earth to rule and reign. This return is called the Second Coming.

The Second Coming is the heralding of the Millennium, a period of time roughly a thousand years in length in which Jesus Christ will personally and physically govern the earth. During this time, Satan will be bound. After the Millennium there will be another season of trial. Satan will be released, and we will prove, once and for all, whose side we are on. Then comes the judgment and the reward. It is toward this moment that we are all headed.

The Day of Judgment is inescapable; however, its pronouncement upon our heads is entirely of our own choosing. We must ask ourselves now: who will we be when we get there? For there to be incomprehensible joy at that judgment, our answer must be that we are servants, friends, and children of the Gods we know. "For this is life eternal" that we might know God, the Eternal Father, and Jesus Christ, whom He hast sent (John 17:3).

This mortal life is the time for us to prepare to meet the Gods; yea, behold the day of this mortal life is the day for us to perform our labors (Alma 12:24; Alma 34:32). We cannot procrastinate forming these relationships with the divine. We must come to an understanding of who They are and who we are in relation to Them. That is the purpose of the gospel and has been since the days of Adam and Eve.

THE GODS I WORSHIP

The doctrines and principles of the gospel, also known as commandments, are not designed to separate us from the Gods, but rather to refine us so that we can approach Them, never to leave Them again. We are here to become heirs of God, joint-heirs with Christ; not to be slaves, but to be students. We are very literally apprentices learning our craft.

Our inheritance as the children of God is to become like Him—not to supplant Him, as the traitor Satan tried to do. Rather, we are to follow the pattern of Jesus Christ, who lives with a singular united purpose to see the will of the Father done, giving all glory to the Father, and in so doing achieving glory for Himself, which in turn furthers the divinity of God.

A daughter that grows to be a mother does not replace her own mother. Rather, she adds upon her mother's titles, making her a grandmother as well as a mother. There is not less love in the world for her, there is more. So it is with God. As we achieve all that He would have us achieve, nothing is taken from Him. Instead, as we gain glory, we add glory to Him. There is no heresy in this; there is only divine heredity.

It is this eventual divine end that gives clarity to mortality. This second estate is for our good, despite the pain of sufferings and sacrifices that plague us here. In order to see that good, we must look beyond our current shallow depth of field and see those whom we worship and why we worship Them. It is only then—when we come to personally know the Godhead, not just facts about Them—that we find our answers.

To know the Father, the Son, and the Holy Ghost is a personal quest that must be undertaken by each of us. No one else can create that relationship for us. While we can, and must, strengthen one another in our efforts to come to know the divine, we alone can present ourselves to be known by Them. Like any relationship, this one requires trust, love, forgiveness, faith, and time.

Wherever we are, we can draw closer to Them. There is no need for distance. We separate ourselves from Them, not the other way around. The Gods call our names homeward; it is we who must learn to listen.

It is possible, even in this mortal state, on this chaotic earth, veiled as we are, to worship the Gods with perfect love. This is the purpose of mortality: to know Them, to love Them, and to become like Them.

The Eternal Father

God the Eternal Father is, as His titles declare, both a god and a father. As a god, He is omnipotent, omnipresent, and omniscient. That is to say, He is almighty, all-powerful, invincible, unstoppable, supreme, universal, present in all places at all times, all-knowing, and all-seeing; He is infinite in His awareness, understanding, insight, and love. As a father, He is a creator, a protector, a founder, a patriarch, a priest, a king, a nurturer, an adviser, a comforter, and literally the father of our spirits.

Our Eternal Father has many names. Elohim is perhaps the most sacred and as such is, out of sacred respect, used the least. He is also called Righteousness, the Almighty, Holiness, and, succinctly, God. While there are many other titles by which He is known, perhaps the most poignant and powerful testimony of His character is that He asks that we call Him Father.

This is not a god who seeks to separate himself from his creations. This is a god who calls after His children throughout every age, reminding us that we belong to His family and that He is our Father. His work and His glory is stated eloquently, to be for "the immortality and eternal life of man" (Moses 1:39). With all of His omnipotent, omnipresent, and omniscient powers, He chooses to spend His everlasting days saving His children.

This makes the Father a god that I can worship without fear. While the blindness of mortality makes obedience difficult, faith, which is trust in action, is something that can be given with completeness. One of His many divine attributes that makes this possible is His inability to lie or to fail. The knowledge that what He says is true, that there is no greater power than His, and that He wields that power for our sakes, makes living the gospel possible.

He asks us to sacrifice, which means to make sacred. He asks us to be obedient, not so that He will have groveling subjects, but so that He can elevate us to holier spheres of ever increasing knowledge, power, and glory. He is love personified.

From before the formation of this mortal proving ground, the Father has been in complete command. He watches over all of us, sending forth His word to us through His Son, the Spirit, and those who follow Them on both sides of the veil. Angels and prophets alike have always administered to all who will give them ear. Their messages are the words of the Father. He is the great organizer, lawgiver, judge, and ruler of all. Life comes from Him. Life has purpose because of Him.

It is to Him that we pray, petition, plead, and give praise. Yet because of the inherited spiritual death of the Fall of Adam and Eve, there is a separation from Him that we cannot cross so long as sin clings to our souls. Knowing that this would be the case, the Father prepared His Son, Jesus Christ, to be our mediator, and thereby Christ became our bridge across this spiritual divide. When we pray, we pray to the Father in the name of the Son.

In every dispensation it is the Father who has introduced the Son to His prophets, thereby establishing not only His divine stamp of approval upon the Son, but also declaring His love for us by providing a divine hierarchical bridge for us to cross. It is His voice and personage that declares, "This is my Beloved Son, hear Him!" (Joseph Smith—History 1:17).

It is through our hearing of the Son that we can come to the Father in this mortality. Spiritual death can be conquered only in this manner. Therefore, while we, out of planned necessity, are temporarily separated from the physical presence of our Father, we are not banished, neglected, or far from Him.

Because spiritual death creates this natural divide, the Father has caused the gospel to be preached, the priesthood to be administered, and eternal ordinances to be provided to all who humbly seek them. Through this gospel, which is the teaching of the Atonement of Jesus Christ, we are able to partake of the blessings of the priesthood. The priesthood uses the keys that unlock the eternal doors that currently bar us from our Father. Theses keys are the ordinances of the gospel. These ordinances include baptism and the Gift of the Holy Ghost, followed by the initiatory, the endowment, the sealing of children to parents, and the sealing of eternal marriages as can only be performed in the holy temples of God.

In the days of the Old Testament washing, anointing, and the presentation of a holy garment were performed at the tabernacle

(Exodus 40:12-13). Today, similar washing, anointing, and sacred undergarments are received in the dedicated temples of God. This ritual is called the initiatory as it is the initial ceremony performed in the temple. The endowment is the next temple ceremony. It is here, in the endowment, where the scriptures are expounded in greater detail, future blessings are promised, and additional covenants to the Father are made; similar to the covenant made at baptism.

To be sealed means that through the authority of the priesthood we can make covenants that last forever both here on earth and in heaven (Matthew 16:19). To be sealed as husband and wife in the temple means that there will be no end to that marriage at death. It is the same with children. To be sealed as a family in the temple is to have a family that is unbroken by the divide of the grave. The temple sealing is the only way that the Father has provided for us to have an eternal family.

THE ETERNAL FATHER

The Father has required that these ordinances be administered to everyone who receives a mortal body. This has been done so that no obstacle will stand between us. Furthermore, as we pass through each successive door, these ordinances allow the Father to heap eternal blessings upon us so that we might continue toward Him with ever-increasing divine strength.

Knowing that it would be logistically impossible for all of His children to participate and receive these required ordinances in mortality, the Father created temples for the living to perform work for those whom we call the dead, but would be more accurately described as members of our family who do not currently have a body.

A physical body is a requirement to participate in the priesthood ordinances. As such, it is a current necessity for the living to do temple work for the dead. Temple work is the shorthand name for performing the ordinances of the temple—the initiatory, endowment, and sealings for families, as well as baptism for the dead and confirmation of the Holy Ghost—for those who have died. This work is done by proxy. For example, a living person would be baptized with the name of the dead in place of their own. In all other respects the ceremony is the same as a baptism for the living. It is in this way that the temple work is done for the deceased. The living temporarily take on the names of the dead to perform the ordinances so that the dead may live forever with all the blessings and covenants available to mankind.

It is clear that resurrected men have the ability to perform priesthood ordinances as well, and one can easily conclude that when the time period of the Millennium envelops the earth, this great work of salvation will be multiplied exponentially. Through the temple work and the promise of the continuation of this work in the resurrection, we can see the fairness of God's plan. All who kept their first estate will be given the opportunity to receive not only an immortal resurrected body, but every required ordinance as well. Ultimately, the only thing that can keep us from returning to our Father is our will not to do so.

This will is called the agency of man. Our agency is given to us by our Father. Our ability to think, reason, decide, and choose what, how, and when we act is so sacred to our Father that He will not remove it from us, not even when we use this agency to rebel against Him and harm His other children. This agency is safeguarded to such an unflinching degree for the singular reason that without it, we could achieve nothing of ourselves and would therefore fail to become like our Father.

This ability to choose for ourselves creates a natural instinct to question all that we encounter. It is in our very nature to be headstrong, rebellious, doubtful, and opinionated. Left to our own devices, these traits would be vices destined to destroy us. However, coupled with the knowledge of the gospel of Jesus Christ, these same traits become divine blessings enabling us to rebel against the false teachings of the world and remain steadfast to the truths taught by the Father.

We must use this agency constantly, as there is "opposition in all things" (2 Nephi 2:11). This does not necessarily mean that there is evil in all things, but rather, that everything has an opposite. There is always a choice to be made in all circumstances.

While we have little control over our circumstances, we do have full control over our characters. That is the blessing of agency and its burden. The Father has made us agents unto ourselves. He has given us the emancipating power to act, not the enslavement of being acted upon (2 Nephi 2:26).

Mortality has purpose. That purpose is progression. Progression is possible only if there is opposition. Opposition gives us our ability to choose. We have been sent here, to this mortal life, to choose good over evil; yet while we are commanded, called, persuaded, and beseeched to choose the good, we are not compelled to do so by our Father. He has given us the ability to recognize good from evil, and He has provided the means by which we can be forgiven when we choose incorrectly. However, because He will not overlook those misplaced choices with any degree of acceptance, there are consequences to our decisions.

We are accountable to Him for our actions, our thoughts, and our desires. He has set a bar of perfection for us to achieve. This bar cannot be reached by any of us. This is not an accident, nor is it malice. The Father requires us to reach for perfection—more accurately described as completion or wholeness—knowing that we will fail to achieve it, but also knowing that in reaching for this celestial bar, we travel farther than we think possible. And although the distance to perfection remains astronomical in our estimations, it is in reality crossed in a single stride of His Son. If we partake of it, the Atonement makes all things possible for us, including our humbled return to the Father in a state of gifted, merciful forgiveness.

Forgiveness, while ultimately being a gift of grace, is nevertheless something that we must strive to earn. Mercy claimeth her own (Alma 42:24). In order to qualify for the salvation of mercy, we must be merciful to others. As much as we ask for forgiveness from the Father, we must offer forgiveness to His other children.

Additionally, forgiveness does not come merely through asking. We must use our ability to act and thereby live a life that draws us closer to our Father and His eternal will for us.

This is the great struggle of mortality: to use our agency to sacrifice the temporal desires of our natural hearts in order to achieve the everlasting blessings of our divine inheritance as the children of God the Father. In theory, there should be no challenge to this. The end result is so clearly greater than anything that we can achieve in rebellion that the very idea of choosing a contrasting ideal, in any form, seems utterly laughable. Yet obedience in mortal life is a very real, daily challenge, and it is purposefully so.

In large part this challenge comes from the simple nature of there being opposition in all things. Furthermore, we have been sent here by our Father to be proven in all things. This means that He is literally trying—otherwise known as testing—our patience and faith in Him. We are here not merely to draw breath, but rather to be proven loyal to the will of the Father. Naturally, this requires trials in life—trials that seem insurmountable but which, once conquered, always reveal themselves to have been for our ultimate growth.

THE GODS I WORSHIP

These natural challenges and circumstances of mortality are further compounded by the fact that we are at war with the invisible, yet fully felt, legions of Satan. He has not forgotten that we stood against him in the courts of the Father, nor has he forgiven us for rejecting his rebellion. He is actively doing all that he can to destroy us by blinding us from the purpose of this life: namely, that we must come to know and return to the Father through the Son. He sought to destroy the work of God the Father then, and he seeks to destroy it now. However, he will fail.

The Father, knowing all things, has given us the divine weapons to wage and win this ongoing war against our fallen brother. The metaphoric atom bomb in our arsenal is the Atonement of Jesus Christ. All other weapons stem from this symbolic nuclear power. The priesthood, faith, prayer, scriptures, prophets, righteousness, preaching of the gospel, truth, and the Holy Ghost clothe us in the divine armor and weaponry forged by the Father for our defense. While at no point has He promised us a transfer from the mortal battlefield to an oasis of peace, He has promised us an ultimate victory over our would-be conquerors.

This ultimate guarantee of success does not mean that mortality will be easy, fair, or understandable. Mortal life is filled with trials, tragedies, atrocities, incurable diseases, and premature deaths that threaten to shatter our confidence in a merciful Father. How can He be fair, loving, and kind when such suffering exists in such overabundance? It is perhaps this question that haunts the mortal mind the most. Where is the justice and the mercy of God when He allows such suffering?

Faith is required to hear the answer: that while this mortal life is all that we can see, feel, and remember, it is but a single stage of the eternal process of our lives. The fairness, the justice, the mercy, the promised rewards for lives devoted to worshiping the Father are only glimpsed in this mortal life. The Father has promised us that the fullness of our blessings comes after we pass through the veil of this mortality. While we have this assurance from the Father, waiting to experience its fruition, is the greatest test of our faith.

However, this does not mean that we do not experience magnificent blessings in this mortality. We are capable of experiencing joy, peace, happiness, contentment, love, and freedom from sin in this stage of life to such a miraculous degree that it defies our ability to produce words to adequately describe them. Indeed, there is great joy to be had in the here and now—consuming joy. Yet the fullest measure of joy that we feel here will seem insignificant compared to what awaits us once we fully return to the Father.

That is the great juxtaposition of mortality. While we are constantly blessed, we are also constantly tested. It is in this dichotomy that we come to understand the profound love of the

Father for us. For in it, we see that the tests are designed to improve us and the blessings are given as rewards for any attempt on our behalf to take those tests. We do not have to be successful in order to be blessed. Instead, we need only to be genuinely willing in order to qualify for blessings.

The very moment we exercise a willingness to choose good, we are blessed for that choice. Our Father is eager to shower us with blessings. Although they are not instantaneous to our view, there is no delay in His rewards. Nor is there an end to His gift giving. He is the ultimate devoted father patiently teaching His infant children how to walk in holy spheres.

These divine strides, longer and more purposeful than we are naturally inclined to pace ourselves with, are required in order to follow the path into eternity. It is a steep, narrow, and long path that leads us through the perils of this mortality, yet it is not an unmarked one.

Since long before the days of Adam and Eve, our Father has labored tirelessly to groom the path, post markers, erect guardrails, and place watchtowers occupied by faithful guardians along the way for our protection and encouragement. We call these divine aids from our Father ordinances, commandments, scriptures, and prophets. Additionally, we have an unfailing compass and the ultimate healer hiking up the trail with us, stride for staggering stride. These ultimate companions furnished to us by the wisdom of our Father are the Holy Ghost and Jesus Christ.

Our Father has always understood that we could not withstand the hike alone. For this reason, divine inspiration is not an isolated moment in our lives. Nor are we extended only one request to follow Him. While there are natural consequences for disobedience that must be overcome for our progression, the

THE ETERNAL FATHER

Father has promised His children that as often as we will repent and try again, He will forgive us. This is the totality of His love for us.

And yet, we must not forget that the Father has also issued us the paternal warning that there is a point when the path we are meant to follow will forever be lost to us. This is not because He removes it, blinds us from finding it again, and refuses to offer directions back to it. Rather, it is because we, His children, can reach a level of stubbornness, otherwise known as sin, in which we have no desire to have anything to do with the path and the Father waiting for us at its victorious height. It is then, when we utterly refuse to climb, and only then, when the divine gifts that have been extended to us cease to function.

The Atonement of Jesus Christ, all powerful as it is, the vanquisher of death in both its bitter forms, will not trump our agency. If we choose to reject the Gods, then we reject Their gifts as well. We have the power to cast ourselves out from Their presence, influence, and association. While Their love remains fixed upon us, we can make ourselves Their enemies. Stunningly, it is possible for us to forge a horrific life for ourselves, devoid of all light and eternal leanings toward the divine.

It is this possibility that gives our Father's warnings such poignant utterances. Knowing the calamity that we could choose to inflict upon ourselves, the Father perpetually calls us far from the edge of our self-imposed banishment. Accordingly, the established guardrails are high; the signposts are succinct and point in one direction. The watchtowers and their occupants stand boldly along the path; they do not sway in the wind; they are firm, built upon unshakable foundations. The compass points in one eternal direction. There is no variance. All are fixed on our salvation.

If we give ear to these gifts of our Father, then no matter how many times we trip and crash mightily to the ground, skinning our knees or breaking our collarbone, and no matter how many times we approach the point of exhausted fainting, the master Healer will always bind us up and carry us onward, if it so be that we desire it. This is the great promise of our Father. We do not need to climb perfectly; we just have to try. He has seen to the rest.

The Father loves us. He loves us to such a perfect degree, He has spared no effort for our sake. Not even His firstborn Son, Jesus Christ. The Father sent His Son to experience every pain imaginable, and millions more that defy our comprehension. He did this for us. Completely understanding our limitations, the Father sent His only limitless Son to pay for our every act of rebellion, to feel our every emotion, to bow under our every suffering so that nothing that mars us in this phase of our lives can go unhealed.

While justice is a fixed law of the eternities, the Father has found a way to circumvent it by producing the equally eternal law of mercy. Coupled together, the rigid requirements of justice and the sweeping compassion of mercy have forged a divine balance for our sakes.

In our Father's plan, justice and mercy exist side by side, thereby creating a judgment that is both just and merciful. This perfect system of law exist through the execution of the Atonement, which simultaneously pays the expensive demands of justice and issues the full measure of mercy without denying the needed representation and execution of both. This is the system of judgment as established by the Father. It is perfection personified.

However, the Father warns us that we have the ability to reject this form of merciful judgment. We do so by rejecting the Atonement. If we reject this crucial element to the Father's way of judging, then we cause the law to revert to a state of pure justice.

This form of judgment, having chosen to cast mercy out, is fixed singularly on the law of justice. In this state, the law, which we choose to inflict upon ourselves, demands punishment for every broken statute in full measurement. And having rejected the Atonement, we alone must pay the eternal price for our every failing, no matter how slight or profound; the fines must be paid to the maximum.

Given the choice between our Father's form of judgment and the judgment of our own creation, it would seem inconceivable that anyone would chose justice over mercy. Yet our Father, who cannot lie, tells us that not only will some choose this unnecessary suffering, but we are just as likely to do the same if left to our own natures.

It is for this reason that we are so often rebuked by Him and by the servants He sends forth to speak for Him. Our Father is correcting our direction now, while we will still listen to His voice. He calls so that we need not cry out in the agony of our own agency. He commands us so that we will not condemn ourselves. For this reason, He has forged a narrow road for us to follow, so that we might not become lost upon it.

With our veiled eyes it is easy to see the Father as a rigid lawgiver, fixated on rudimentary rules, forever denying us the pleasures of this life. But the reality of His character and purpose is the exact opposite.

He is not keeping His children under His thumb; He is lifting us onto His shoulders. His aim is not to lessen us; it is to magnify us. He did not forge this perfect plan for the sake of creating rules; rather, His plan is to refine us into celestial rulers.

This is the true nature of God. With all of His infinite power and incomprehensible might, His chief characteristic is eloquently repeated in every age to be love (1 John 4:16). The Great Spiritual Creator of all that we know of existence, the power of its creation and continuation, the God who is worthy of every lofty, divine, unspeakable title, asks us to call Him, "Father."

Truly, He is a God of greatness, for He is our loving Eternal Father in Heaven. He can be trusted with completeness, worshiped without wavering fear, loved limitlessly, and approached always.

His ways are of justice and mercy. His plan is the Atonement. His work is our salvation from death, even our immortality and eternal life. His Son is Jesus Christ, whom He sent to His rebellious children to save us from ourselves. His mighty messenger to His children is the Holy Ghost, who is without limit to teach and testify. He is our Father. He is love.

Jesus The Christ

Because of the Eternal Father's infinite love for us, He prepared, anointed, and sent His only perfect Son, Jesus the Christ, to be our redemptive savior. Never has more been required of any man than of Jesus Christ. A single failing on His part and all would have been irrevocably lost. The strength, devotion, courage, and sheer volume of love that was forged in Jesus's being defies mortal comprehension or duplication.

Already a god, Jesus left His eternal throne for a tabernacle of clay, risking a lifetime of temptation and persecution the likes of which none of us will ever experience (Mosiah 3:5). His purpose was perpetually singular. It was not to gain glory, power, or dominion over the earth He created under the direction of the Father, nor to take command of the peoples He had overseen from its beginning. Rather, Jesus's mortal life was one of total servitude.

Jesus used His understanding of the universe to teach others of their potential. He manifested His mighty priesthood in healing miracles. He commanded the elements to build faith. And He shattered death itself in order to give life. No wonder the Father declared that He was well pleased in His Son (Matthew 3:17). Having absolute power, Christ uses it with absolute perfection.

And it's no wonder that when the great plan of salvation was presented to us in the first estate, even then we looked to our eldest brother, the Firstborn of God, and trusted Him with our salvation. We understood then that we would have to leave a perfect sphere of safety in the courts of our Father to risk a life of temptation and pain. We must have shuddered under the fear of that risk. We were not blind to it; we had been prepared for it. Trusting our Father, yes, but fearing ourselves all the same, we would have held lingering doubts, ripe for the Rebel to strike upon. We knew we would make mistakes here. We knew we would sin. We knew the consequences of those sins.

We must have had an idea, too, of what physical pain might be like when housed in mortal flesh. We were aware of sickness, of suffering, of the unfairness of the elements we were volunteering to become subject to. We knew there would be poverty, injustices, tyrants, and unfathomable losses. For the plan to work, it had to be real. The choices and the consequences had to be answerable upon our own heads. We knew that. We also knew Jehovah.

When the Father presented the Firstborn as the means by which we would all be saved, that was enough for us. Knowing that our Brother, Jehovah, whom we knew so well, had volunteered to see it done, we trusted Him absolutely. If Jehovah said it, He would do it. Our faith in His faithfulness was so absolute that we did not quiver in doubt, we did not murmur in fear; rather, we shouted with joy and wept in wonder, because we knew that He would not fail us. Knowing the staggering odds against us, we, nevertheless, shouted for joy in the certain knowledge that no odds could overcome our Brother.

Our faith in Jehovah was so secure that millions of our brothers and sisters came before He was even born. For thousands of years they came to this earth before the Atonement was completed. Before Jehovah drew His first fragile breath as a newborn baby, they came trusting that one day that divine child would be born, and that child would grow into the man who would walk voluntarily into a garden and take upon Himself all of the sins, sickness, and sufferings of every life, and in turn create salvation for us all.

THE GODS I WORSHIP

They came to this mortality, experienced all of it, and died, crossing into a realm that could not be escaped until death was conquered by the Son who had yet to be born. They waited in that realm not with howling laments of regret and doubts, but with echoing songs of praise that when Christ was born, He would not fail them.

There were but a precious few who would live their mortality side by side with the Brother they had always trusted, and even fewer still who would recognize their God in their midst. Yet they too came in their day filled with faith that the Atonement would be accomplished.

These endless generations that were born and died before the days when Christ's victorious labors were completed were not abandoned by time. Their lives were not wasted waiting. Nor were they spent in a darkness without revelation or salvation to guide and uplift them. So perfect was, and is, our Brother that while He had yet to come to this mortality, the guarantee of His perfection was already in place. Repentance and forgiveness were already possible through His name. He had yet to bleed from every pore, yet the blood of the Lamb of God had already sanctified His people (Mosiah 16:6).

Adam and Eve were the first to be placed in this mortal sphere. They were the first to sin and fall, and they were the first to be saved by the Atonement of Christ. Eve had not yet had Seth, who would in turn produce the lineage that would bring forth the promised Messiah; yet her future mortal grandson, some thousands of years away, already had the power to heal her wounds of body and soul and reunite her eternally with the Father. Given a witness of this, Eve rejoiced, claiming boldly and prophesying accurately that all the trials of life were a worthy price to pay in order to know again our most trusted Brother, Jesus the Christ.

Adam and Eve spent all their long lives declaring the truth of the salvation of Christ to their children. Many of those children in turn declared their own witness to all who would listen. Wherever they were sent, to whatever continent, culture, or clime, those blessed with a testimony of Christ devoted their lives to declaring that salvation would come in the meridian of time; and even more gloriously, no one had to wait for that time to come in order to be saved. They could be saved now. Already, Christ had made it possible to live.

The prophets were so certain of this great future event that many of them spoke of it in the past tense. (Mosiah 3:13). To them it was as if it had already happened. All the prophets from Adam onward declared with absolute conviction that Jehovah—their Great Creator, the Lord God, God Himself, the Firstborn, the Savior of Mankind—would walk the earth in mortal flesh healing the injured, teaching the ignorant, and completing the Atonement for all mankind, both in the Garden of Gethsemane and upon the cross at Golgotha.

Before time cut hills out of the land, before gardens were planted, before names were assigned to them by man, before the Roman Empire existed to conquer a chosen people, already the prophets of God knew what would happen in those now holy lands. Thousands of years before a cave was purchased as a tomb, it was known that this tomb would be the first to fail—that death itself would fail. Its chain would shatter, never again to hold sway over life.

These prophecies would be accomplished by Jehovah when He came to earth through a mortal mother. He would live as a mortal man, and yet He was more than a mortal. His father would be the Father. He would become the Only Begotten. He was blessed with both the frailty of mortality through His mother and the power of divinity through His father. This utterly unique parentage allowed Christ to live as a mortal man, subject to all the weaknesses and temptations that come with mortality, but also to be endued with the powers of the divine.

Chiefly, Christ had the power and authority that no other mortal could obtain. He, the Great Creator, voluntarily separated His spirit from His mortal body on the cross, commanding His spirit back to His Father (Luke 23:46). Furthermore, in three days' time, Jesus commanded His spirit into His now resurrected body and thereby completed His great, endless work for all of mankind.

We knew this would happen before the earth was formed. This knowledge infused us with the courage to be faithful, obedient, and bold in our first estate. Adam and Eve knew it before they had their first child. Their knowledge caused them to rejoice, to prophesy, and to live in devoted righteousness throughout their second estate.

The Atonement of Jesus Christ was a resounding, universal, infinite, time-defying success. From before the foundations of the earth, Jesus the Christ was the promised Messiah. The prophets spoke of Him in the past tense because they knew He would not fail them, and they were right.

From its beginning, Jesus's mortal life was designed to be a humble one. Born in a Bethlehem stable, most likely little more than a cave, He was swaddled and lain meekly in a manger under the protective care of two of the most trusted mortals in all of history. Although legions of angels trumpeted His long-awaited arrival, stars erupted in the heavens, wonders of light appeared around the globe, and scores of prophecies were fulfilled with lifesaving perfection, the immediate countryside saw nothing of note in the newborn babe. All the signs that the great God of the earth had at last been born upon it went predominantly unseen by those nearest to His holy birth. So it was with the rest of Jesus's mortality.

While some left everything straightaway to follow Him, the rest of the region saw only a troublesome man in Jesus of Nazareth, thinking Him little more than a fly buzzing about the ear of a horse. He was a nuisance at best, a rebel at worst. He was dismissed outright by most. His teachings were rejected, His miracles attributed to the devil as tricks meant to lead the people astray. He was mocked, spat upon, denied, and cast out at every turn. And yet the great Lord was not swayed from His mission of love by the hatred and envying of others.

Loved by only a few, mocked by most, hated by the rest, Christ nonetheless went forth in perfect love. And as He promised, He remained perfect. He did not fall. He did not stumble. He did not give way to self-interest, self-doubt, or selfishness.

The enemy of us all was waiting for Him. Satan went after Jesus with a precision and persistence that none of us will ever understand. Everything, absolutely everything, was dependent on Christ. It takes little imagination to understand that every weapon in the arsenal of Satan was unleashed upon this humble man of Galilee. Never has anyone been hated more than Jehovah by the fallen Lucifer.

From the very beginning of mortality, Satan has done all that he can to snuff out the divine life that would bring life to all others. In the Garden of Eden, Satan slithered like the subtle serpent, twisting the words of the Gods in on themselves to manipulate the understandings of Adam and Eve. On the surface, he appears to have gained a small victory over them. But the reality is that Satan has never understood the mind of God the Father (Moses 4:6). He thought to trick Adam and Eve out of their blessings. He succeeded only in speeding up a process that was a planned eventuality, and even that success can be debated.

Adam and Eve were always going to partake of the forbidden fruit. That's why the tree had been planted in the Garden by God Himself. The Father was not surprised by the tree's appearance. He was not afraid of its fruit. He was not unnerved by the possibility that His children might accidentally partake of it. He told them, even in His commandment not to eat it, that it was their choice whether they would do so or not.

No other commandment has been given with such a carefully worded caveat. It was forbidden fruit, yes; yet, Adam and Eve were allowed to eat it, so long as they understood the consequence would be death. Conversely, Adam and Eve had also been taught that they needed knowledge in order to fulfill the other commandments of God, to multiply and replenish the earth. This paradox of command allowed for the required opposites and oppositions that alone can create the opportunity for choice.

It was always the plan for them to choose to eat of the fruit, because that is the choice of life itself. We come here knowing we will die, and we are willing to die in order that we might know good from evil. With that knowledge we are at last able to multiply and replenish the earth as God would have us do.

Satan did not understand this then, and he strives to make us misunderstand it now. He would have us see the requisite paradox of the forbidden fruit as a sign against the good character of our Father. The enemy would cite unfairness and strive to make us doubt the motivations of such a test, perhaps simply because he failed to use it to overthrow Adam and Eve's chances.

When Eve came to understand that the fruit offered the only way to gain the knowledge she needed to be faithful and not just ignorantly obedient, she found the courage to partake of the fruit, accepting death so that she could live.

When Adam learned of Eve's choice, fully understanding her consequences, he made a carefully thought-out choice of his own. Adam chose death too, so that he could live his life with his wife. They both ate so that we, their mortal offspring, could come into being upon this earth (2 Nephi 2:25). That is what they chose. The nobility of their choice, the totality of their sacrifice for children they had not yet borne, is a succinct summary of their goodness.

Adam and Eve were no random people, haphazardly chosen at whim to be the first placed on this earth by the Father. They were chosen for their righteousness. Adam was the archangel Michael. While we know less about Eve's accomplishments in the first estate, it is clear by her acts in this second estate that Eve was most likely second to only one other woman, just as Adam was most likely second in righteousness only to Christ. To be the Mother of All Living is a title that can be bested only by the title her great-granddaughter, Mary, would eventually be blessed with, the Mother of God.

Consequently, Adam and Eve would have been very well known by their fallen, hateful, vengeful brother, Lucifer. Because of the veil, Adam and Eve could not remember their first estate; however, Satan has no such binding on his memory.

Upon finding these two most precious children of God innocently going about their way in the Garden of Eden, Satan attacked them as the enemy he is. Although subtle in his manipulations, he was nonetheless relentlessly determined to cause them suffering. So he pressed until at last Eve, having looked for some time upon the fruit and the gaining of the knowledge it represented, chose the consequences of death as an acceptable price for progress.

Satan, not knowing that this was the will of God, rejoiced at his perceived triumph. He did not understand that Adam and Eve needed the knowledge of good and evil that could only become theirs by implementing their divine rights of agency. He did not understand that it was for this very purpose that the Garden had been planted.

Knowledge, coupled with accountability, gave Adam and Eve, and all of their descendants by rights of inheritance, the ability to choose the Atonement unto salvation and eternal life. This was the design of the Father, put in place before He sent His Son Jehovah to oversee the formation of the earth and all that dwell upon it, in it, and around it.

As promised, death entered the world, both spiritually and physically, when Adam and Eve partook of the fruit. However, so too did the promise of the Atonement. Realizing that he had failed to thwart the Gods in this instance, and being punished for his attempts to do so, Satan bent all of his wrath upon the destruction of the children of Adam and Eve, including his most hated brother, the Great Jehovah, Jesus Christ.

It was with this purpose that Satan made an oath with Cain to slay Abel. Assuming that Christ would be born through righteous Abel's lineage, Satan attempted to execute Christ before He was even born, thereby destroying the Atonement and plunging all souls into a state of unending captivity to sin and its consequences.

While Abel did die by the wicked hand of his corrupted brother Cain, God nevertheless raised up another righteous son to Adam and Eve. Seth was born in the exact likeness of his father, Adam. His line survived through millennia of upheavals, wars, temptations, apostasies, restorations, and wanderings, until the appointed hour, in the prophesied manner, when an angel came to the young woman called Mary and heralded her as the Mother of God.

Having failed for thousands of years to kill off the ancestors of Christ, Satan would have redoubled all his efforts upon this most holy of virgins and her espoused husband. Mary and Joseph, like Adam and Eve, were clearly of the highest caliber of spirits in both the first and second estates.

Mary, a mortal woman chosen to be the mother of the God she had worshiped all her life, and Joseph, a righteous man of great faith tasked with being the stepfather of God's Only Begotten Son, were not crushed by the unrelenting pressures of Satan. They were righteous people, honest and humble. They believed, obeyed, and fulfilled the words of the angels that were brought to them time and again.

Every warning was heeded, every lesson learned, every command obeyed. When the time came, Mary and Joseph were exactly where the ancients prophesied they would be, laying the great Jehovah in a manger, bearing an eyewitness account of the unquenchable love of God for all His children.

The love Jesus had for His mortal parents would most likely not be understood by any child. He had been born to save them. He had condescended to leave all the powers, safeties, and splendors of an eternal court in order to be born in a cave meant for animals. The King of kings, the Lord of lords, the Creator of the created, had chosen the most humble of circumstances to come into the world as a fulfillment of His own word to His own prophets. His birth was a sign long foretold.

So were His parents. As much as we trusted Him to come into this world so we could be saved by His perfect life, Christ must have trusted that these two faithful souls would not fail Him either.

The virgin mother, the faithful stepfather—together, these two mortals were tasked with the raising of the Messiah. This most extraordinary of blessings and burdens would have required a degree of righteousness that few mortals have ever achieved. Constantly on their spiritual guard, Mary and Joseph rose to the foretold callings and raised the Son of God in their precious care. They did not fail Him, and He in turn did not fail them.

Time and again, in the early years of Christ's mortality, when He was perhaps at His most vulnerable as a small babe and child, Joseph and Mary had to flee to safety from the relentless attacks of Satan's mortal minions. They were warned in dreams, conversed with angels, and were ever prompted by the Holy Ghost; and each time, with each exodus and each arrival, this little divine family fulfilled scripture. Prophecy after prophecy was made into the facts of history, proving once again that Satan doesn't understand the mind of God.

Every attempt to thwart the Father or the Son has always failed. Satan's powers, though very real, are nothing to the designs of the Gods. While we can give in, stumble, fall, or outright betray the plans of God, we cannot prevent them from being fully accomplished.

All we can do is keep ourselves from participating in their glorious fulfillment. Yet this need not be the fate of any of God's children. The Son has seen to that.

When the time had come for the Messiah to start His earthly ministry, He went out into the wilderness to fast and pray in order to prepare Himself for what He knew was coming. It comes as no surprise that when those forty days were over, Satan was there to tempt Him. It also comes as no surprise that Christ did not give in to those temptations.

The brothers, so long at war with one another, faced off once again. And as promised in the Garden of Eden to Eve, the Mother of All Living, Satan had only the power to bruise Christ's heel, nipping like a dog after His ankles, whereas Christ would crush Satan's head once and for all through the perfection of the Atonement (Genesis 3:15).

This miracle is illustrated time and again in Christ's mortal life. We see it in the encounter in the wilderness; in the secret, illegal night trials; in the false judgment; in the beatings, whippings, crowning of thorns; in the rushed crucifixion; and ultimately, in the empty tomb.

Despite everything against Him—from the ordinary nature of mortal life to the extraordinary relentless personal attacks of Satan, to the doubts of otherwise faithful men and the outright hatred of the wicked—Christ remained perfect. He spent every waking moment of His ministry teaching, through word and more powerfully by deed.

His works, despite being thousands of years old, have survived miraculously through the fall, ruination, and recreation of civilization itself. And it is not just one witness that testifies that Jesus Christ actually did what was prophesied He would do; it is millions of witnesses.

Just as the ancients were able to testify of Christ's ministry and miracles in the past tense, so too can the moderns testify of Christ in the present tense. Such is the eternal nature of His life's work. There is no beginning nor end. Jesus the Christ truly is the Alpha and the Omega. He is the life-force of all mortals and the only way back to the eternal realms from which we hail. Repentance and resurrection come through His name alone. Jesus the Christ, the foretold Messiah, the divine Jehovah, is the Great Redeemer.

It is His life, His teachings, His miracles, His love, and His Atonement that gives meaning to life. Even more spectacularly, it is His Atonement that makes life itself possible. Had He failed, the purposes of the Father would have failed, and all things would have ceased. But this did not happen.

Christ was victorious, and we have been given the promised life. Repentance, forgiveness, resurrection, salvation, and everlasting life with a family of unending love belongs to all who would have it. The Firstborn of God the Eternal Father, Jesus Christ, calls to all the world with the trumpets of eternal victory. Those trumpets will never fall silent, nor will His triumph ever fall by the wayside.

Christ is not limited. There is no beginning or end to His power or His place in the plan of the Father. Neither is there an end to His divinely perfect Atonement. It is as eternal as it is infinite. There is no numerical quantity at which its quota will fail. It does not work only up to a certain point. It is not the luck of the draw, nor is it the birthright of the few. Christ lived His mortal life as He has ever lived, in obedience to our Father with love unfeigned for all of us.

It is this love, patterned after the love of our Father, that Jesus Christ utilized with infinite power to fulfill all righteousness. Jesus is the very plan of God. The Father calls this plan the Plan of Salvation. Powerfully, He did not name it the Plan of Damnation. It was not created to cull out the throngs of His children from His royal courts on high. It was created to save us. And from the very beginning, starting with Adam and Eve, the plan—Our Savior, Jesus Christ—has done so.

We see His salvation most powerfully in repentance and resurrection, but He is so much more than the conqueror of death.

He is with us in life. It is He who takes the mortal burdens from our shoulders that would otherwise crush us. It is He who weeps with us in the depths of our bitter mourning. It is He who presses a cool hand to our feverish foreheads in our sufferings. It is He who whispers a gentle lullaby in the nights of our terror. And it is He who stands with us when all others have abandoned our cause.

This is the full measure of the Atonement, of the perfect love of Christ. Having endured the Garden of Gethsemane and again the cross of Golgotha, not only does Christ know all things, He has experienced all things, and He has done so for a purpose. Our Elder Brother, through His own isolated suffering, has mastered the art of empathetic healing. This was not a coincidence. It was the calculated purpose of the Atonement.

We will be forever indebted to His love and care, and yet He does not ask for an impossible tax to be paid. Instead, He asks that we come unto Him because He is "mighty to save" (Doctrine and Covenants 133:47).

He stands at the door and knocks so that He can show us the way unto life. He has won the great inheritance for Himself, yet He holds the gate open, beckoning us to join Him as joint-heirs (Romans 8:16–17). And when we heed those divine calls, He rejoices with the host of the heavens over every single life.

Conversely, He weeps over our stubbornness, lamenting that we will not let Him pay our debts but instead insist on remaining enslaved to our self-induced bondage. He groans within Himself at our wickedness and warns that if we do not repent we will have to suffer as He did, which suffering caused Him to tremble and shake and bleed at every pore for the agony of it (Doctrine and Covenants 19:16–18). His voice is as a flaming sword and sharp as lightning to those who refuse to be saved by Him.

To those who fail this second estate, who knowingly choose the blood-soaked standard of Satan over the Father's glowing banner of salvation, the Messiah of mankind will seem to be terrible in His greatness. At His return, He will bring healing in His wings to those who have sought it, and destruction to those who have refused it.

While some will praise the heavens at His arrival, others will wish to crawl beneath the earth in shame. But in that day, all will confess, no matter whose side they have aligned themselves with, that Jesus is the Christ (Philippians 2:10–11).

Agency will not vanish at the Second Coming of the Lord Jesus Christ, but all doubt will. No mortal eye will look upon Him without recognition. Nations will be converted in a day. All will bow before Him, for He is the Son of God, the Savior of Mankind, our Brother, Jehovah, Jesus the Christ. And in that day, we will know what Adam and Eve knew: that the joy of our redemption through Christ our Lord was worth all we endured in this mortality. When we see Him again, we will love Him and be loved by Him as we cannot now comprehend.

The Holy Ghost

All of the certainties of the character of divinity are not creations of blind, desperate hope. The Gods have not been created by man as a means of sparking light in the darkness. Religion is not a cloak of lies to smother out suffering. It is not an opiate, a fairy tale, or a necessary psychological bandage. The Gods are real. So are Their works and glory. The Father and the Son watch over us with protective interest, unflinching love, and devout callings to return to Them. We know this because of the Holy Ghost.

THE GODS I WORSHIP

There are evidences to satisfy the mortal mind, but the convincing power of converted conviction does not come from facts and figures; it comes from the invisible whispering of the God called the Holy Ghost. Ironically, of the Three, He is the God we know the least about, yet have the most personal, interactive, and frequent communications with.

He does not have a resurrected body of flesh and bone as the Father and Son do. He is a personage of spirit, which means that He has form and substance. However, not being bound by the confines of a body, the Holy Ghost is able to be in all places at once. He, like the other members of the Godhead, knows all things.

Yet while He is often described as the Comforter, He does not possess the same personal experience as Jesus Christ and cannot succor us as the Savior can (Alma 7:12–13). Therefore, it is the Holy Ghost's primary role to bring us unto Christ and His healing Atonement.

The Spirit, as He is most frequently called, spends His divine existence guiding the mortal heart and mind back to the divine. His purpose is to instruct us, protect us, comfort us, and, when needed, rebuke us into the ways of Christ. The Spirit can be trusted completely.

His entire aim is to contradict false teachings by dispersing the purity of the doctrines and principles of the gospel of Jesus Christ to all who will listen. He does this with a soft voice, most often inaudible. His voice comes as a feeling, a warmth, or a thought. However, when necessary, He can speak in a voice as clear as a bell and piercing as electricity. He is, in a simple phrase, mankind's best friend.

If we live righteously, the Holy Ghost will be our constant companion. He has the ability to breach the veil, causing the eternal light of Jesus Christ to stream into our lives. While He will not direct us in all things and thereby circumvent our agency, He will guide and inspire us in all necessary matters.

This does not mean that if we are living righteously, no harm, tragedy, or injustice will befall us. It means that when the natural perils of life do assault us, including the myriad of undeserved travesties, we are not alone.

Indeed, it is often at our worst moments that we feel the divine presence of the Spirit most clearly. In our desperation, we actively still the chaos of our minds specifically to hear the eternal whisperings of divinity we otherwise take for granted.

Pain, fear, sickness, doubt, and loss cause us to look for the relief given by the Spirit, who is so adept at administering comfort that He wears the divine title of the Comforter. While bitter pains and emotions often bring us to Him, these ailments of body and soul are the opposites of His personal qualities. Rather, it is in His influence that we can displace pain for peace.

The Comforter's chief characteristics are, firstly, to be a testifier of the truth of the Savior and Master Healer, Jesus Christ; secondly, to instill in us the fruit of the Spirit: love, joy, peace, longsuffering, gentleness, goodness, faith, meekness, and temperance (Galatians 5:22–23). Like the moon reflecting the light of the sun, we too take on divine qualities of light and majesty as we strive to align our lives to the guidance and gravitational pull of the Holy Ghost.

The more we attempt to spend time with this most accessible of Gods, the more He is able to refine us into reflecting the light of Christ—not only into our own lives, but into the lives of those who look upon us. In this act of testimony transference, we are able to participate, in a small way, in the divine pattern of the Godhead. While each of us remains a distinct individual, we are united in our cause for the betterment of mankind.

This, perhaps, is the most significant gift and function of the Holy Ghost. Not only does He have the ability to teach and influence us to follow better paths, He can inspire us to change the quality of our desires from singular selfishness to universal selflessness. He teaches us to live for more than ourselves.

Notably, as we draw closer to the Spirit's way of living, we find that our natures become kinder, gentler, and quicker to serve, and we are far more prone to smile, laugh, and enjoy the company of others.

This natural inclination to be happy and in good humor is a witness of the Spirit's own personality. He is not a morose, haunting ghost, stirring in the shadows or rattling chains in the proverbial attic, bemoaning a life he does not have. He is a God of power, purpose, and self-possession, one who is prone to—and indeed, the inspirer of—all of the lofty qualities we reverently call humanity.

It is He who inspires the very best in us, from the simplest acts of kindness to the grandest works of art. All things that elevate mankind closer to our true selves as children of God the Father are germinated by the workings of the Spirit. His influence never wanes. Wherever there is a spark of goodness, even just as a dim desire, He is there to influence, teach, and comfort. Without Him, there would be no conversion to Christ and His teachings in any quarter of the world.

All of mankind has the inherent ability and right to interact with the Holy Ghost. As infants, we come into this world in a state of innocence, having been forgiven of any sins we may have accumulated in the first estate. We enter this second estate with no marks against us, only blessings (Doctrine and Covenants 93:38).

We are not born plagued by the sins of our fathers, nor are we damned by the transgression of Adam and Eve. We alone are responsible for the lives we live. Because of this, the Spirit is with us from a young age to help guide us into becoming agents unto ourselves. With the exception of those who, due to mental health conditions and illnesses, are not accountable for their actions, all other mortals must take responsibility for their actions, thoughts, and desires.

God the Father has established that the age of accountability—meaning the time at which His children have progressed to a state capable of reasoning and choice—is eight years old (Doctrine and Covenants 68:27). From that point forward, the Father sees us as being capable of making choices. It is also from this point that He has made it possible for His children to be baptized and confirmed with the Gift of the Holy Ghost.

THE HOLY GHOST

The Father expects much of us from an early age; yet He also blesses us, if we are willing, with the constant companionship of a God, the Holy Ghost. Here we see, yet again, the love of our Father for us.

All of mankind, regardless of race or religion, has the ability to be influenced by the Holy Ghost throughout our lives. However, this interaction is limited in comparison to the Gift of the Holy Ghost. The Gift of the Holy Ghost is the ordinance that immediately follows baptism and is sometimes called the second baptism or the baptism of fire (Matthew 3:11). It is a purifier and a sign and covenant between the Father and His children of His love to us and our commitment to Him.

The Gift of the Holy Ghost comes with responsibilities and is conditional upon our obedience in adhering to those responsibilities. From the outset, the gift is not bestowed upon us, but rather we are invited to receive it. The responsibility is on us to live our lives in harmony with the nature and purposes of the Holy Ghost and not merely to be a passive partaker in His influence, as we had been before.

When we strive to honor these increased commitments and covenants, we are endued with the right to have the Spirit with us always. We are given this right when we remember Jesus the Christ, keep His commandments, and are willing to wear His name as a sign for others to follow toward their own salvation into the waters of baptism and the holy temple ordinances. This magnificent divine contract between the Father and His children exists for the continual purpose of achieving our immortality and eternal lives. As we are blessed, so too is the world.

The Gift of the Holy Ghost is not an exclusive gift bestowed on a chosen few or won as a rare prize. Nor is it a hidden treasure, coveted and covertly kept from the rest of the world. The gift is a divine one meant for all the children of the Father to partake in.

No mortal method of payment can secure this gift. Instead, a broken heart and contrite spirit are what lead to this most treasured of blessings (3 Nephi 9:20). Consequently, the purchase price is also the rewarded blessing. As we humble ourselves and desire to be taught by the divine, we offer the ancient sacrifices upon the proverbial altars that sanctify and qualify us to become joint-heirs with Christ.

It is in this great life pursuit of joyful, willing obedience to the designs of the Father that we become most like the Gods. It is also this pursuit that is so fundamentally difficult to sustain in our mortality.

We have been blessed with big personalities and ramrod strength of will. We are not inherently passive, and we are not quick to be persuaded. The more we are pushed into a corner, the fiercer we naturally fight to stand at the center. When we are presented with solutions, we squint our eyes at the formulas that produced them, not trusting the answers if we did not come by them ourselves.

These inherent conditions of mankind sharpen the double-edged sword of our natures. Every quality can be seen as a boon or a burden. However, the ability to stand by a truth the rest of the world does not acknowledge, to hold it fast, nurture it, and preach it to that same naysaying world, requires these very attributes of rebellion, stubbornness, self-possession, and doubt. It is the Holy Ghost that refines us by honing the sharpened blade of our natures, not to our harm but to our healing.

Through the tutoring of the Spirit, our mortal natures become our strength, not our weakness. No matter how frail we are in any or all aspects of our lives, He can teach us to use those same traits to become the very best version of ourselves. Indeed, it is through the influence of the Spirit that we are made whole or perfect.

THE HOLY GHOST

Perfection itself is not a life lived without flaw, smudge, or chipping. For mere mortals such as ourselves, perfection is about completion. The ability to endure, the desire to achieve, the willingness to try again, and the hope that next time we'll do better—these are the qualities of perfection. Such a life is achievable by all of the Father's children. But it is not easy. And it will not happen within the confines of mortality alone.

In fact, the vast majority of the Father's children will not find the doctrine of His Son's Atonement in this life. If they do hear it, the probability that they will recognize the message as the truth sent from the heavens is slight. The realities of this phase of our lives is that divine communications, while meant for all, will find the ears of only a few.

These mathematical odds, so wildly stacked against the creation of the Gods, seem at first to be the major failing of an otherwise perfect plan. However, this is only the case when seen from a mindset that mortality is the beginning and end of our progress. It is not.

We chose to come to mortality while knowing that some would be born into a life in which temple covenants were inherited and others would spend all their mortal lives without hearing a word of the Plan of Salvation. We understood that our every waking day could be one of tribulation and hardships the likes of which other mortals would never experience. Yet we all came. Why?

We came because our Father's Plan of Salvation, seen through to perfection by Our Savior, is not limited in its scope to saving only those rare few who find it in mortality. His plan will save all of His children who will let it save them (Moses 5:9). This means that every single one of us, whether born into a knowledge of the truth or kept from it all of our mortal lives, will be given the same opportunity to gain knowledge, receive ordinances, and choose the better part by uniting ourselves to the will of the Gods.

No child of God that seeks for these things will be denied them. Furthermore, every single one of us will at some point come to know the truth of all things. Consequently, we will all reach a point in our lives where we will make a final, everlasting choice of whose side we are truly on. Most will not make this choice in this mortal time frame, yet there will be no penalty, no weighted scales, no grading on a curve that lessens their reward. This is why the Plan of Salvation is perfect and why it is called the Great Plan of Happiness, for it does not spawn misery; rather, it is the source of eternal joy (Alma 42:8).

In this plan, simply understood as the Atonement of Christ, perfection becomes possible for us all. It also becomes an active choice, a matter of agency.

The circumstances of our lives—birthplace, gender, social and economic class, cultural background, sexual orientation, upbringing, family situation—are not the deciding factors of our salvation. Our will is the only deciding factor.

We choose to follow God or not. That is the glory of the plan. All other trappings of mortality are stripped away. It is our heart, our desire, our longing to return to the Gods that ultimately saves us. This is the great hope that the Holy Ghost gives us in this mortality to both cling to and be comforted by.

Life, eventually, is fair.

Without this hope, borne into our souls by the subtle impressions of the Spirit with more weight than all the scientific proofs in the world, there would appear to be little reason for life. It could be easily argued, as many do, that we are simply born, live, and die, with no purpose, no direction, and no reward waiting for us on the other side of the grave.

Life, they say, is just what we see. For some it is good; for others it is hell on earth. It is simply the luck of the draw, and then it is over. Mortality, to some, is so obviously unfair in all its facets that many have given up in the face of it. Many more, while they continue, do so with only temporary rewards in mind, not believing that there could be more. Mercifully, the Holy Ghost teaches us that there is so much more to life than this narrow world view.

For those whose mortal clocks are wound down in such constantly clouded circumstances, the Spirit teaches that their every experience in mortality will be for their everlasting good. Every trial faced—even the ones we fail—teach us, build us, and create within us character that will in time sustain us throughout all eternity.

This is the miracle of divine knowledge. It can be a grim life. For it is, after all, a hard test. But there is hope and peace and a guarantee of restful reward.

While we have not been asked to take upon us the sins of others, as Christ did, we will—

here and in the life beyond the grave—need to have compassion, sympathy, and empathy with, for, and toward others.

Can any of us pass through this "vale of tears" that we call mortality without developing compassion for others (Psalms 84:6, Douay-Rheims Bible)? Knowing how often we fell, how easily we gave in to sin, and how painful it was to stand again, we will love with a perfection that could only have been forged through our own imperfections.

The Father has told us that He has deliberately given us weakness so that we can be made strong (Ether 12:27). This mortal life, all of it, can be seen as a form of weakness. Our blinded memories, our limited understandings, and our hardships, borne with varying degrees of success, are the building blocks of divinity.

It was understood from the beginning that we would fail. It was also understood from the beginning that we could succeed. This is the point of mortality: to come here, to live, to stumble and fall, and to use the Atonement, now or on the other side of the veil, to become redeemed and receive all that the Father offers.

This is the glorious message of the Spirit of God. There is purpose, reason, hope, compassion, endless love, total understanding, and patience for us, from our Father, our Savior, and the Holy Ghost. They are not our enemies. They are not sitting with giant demerit boards, carefully marking down our every failing, ensuring that every sin, stumbling, and stubbornness is counted against us here and throughout eternity. They are our family.

And while They know our every flaw, Their knowledge is that of master healers who study ailments in order to cure them. They are here for us in mortality, whether we ever notice Them or not. And They are most certainly there for us throughout the continuation of our lives beyond this mortal sphere.

We were sent to this second estate to be tested in all things and to prove ourselves. That proof does not always come here. For some it will, because they are born with the needed knowledge at hand to be tested and tried here and now. For those who do not have that knowledge, the trial of our loyalty comes later. Yet for all of us, no matter our circumstances, this life will be for our ultimate good.

Every spark of knowledge, every scar of experience, every moment of greatness, every ounce of kindness, every longing for more peace, every tear-filled night, every joy-filled day will combine to give us an experience that could not have been gained in any other way. And when, with all of our mortal lives having been played out, we kneel before our Savior, we will have the chance to declare that it was all worth it. All of it.

It is then that we are perfected. It is then, having known the bitterness of doubt, that we will truly know the sweetness of the knowledge of God's love for us. Eventually, every knee will bow before the God who paid the price for this perfection, and every tongue will confess that He is the Christ.

In that day, we will all know the same truth. However, we will not all make the same choice. Some will choose, as others chose in the first war, to stand against the Gods. Their fates will be the same as the fallen host of Lucifer. All others will choose to allow salvation and the greatest heights of exaltation to be crowned upon their heads.

This is the miracle of the Spirit: to know this truth, to feel it in our darkest hours, to be gifted with the foreknowledge of eternity. It is this knowledge that compels those who have found this truth to preach the gospel's light to all the darkened world.

For while we cannot dispel sin, vanquish suffering, or balance the scales of mortal justice, we can declare the everlasting divine truth that hope is real, God's justice and mercy are in perfect harmony, and nothing will be lost, denied, or lessened to any and all of God's children.

We all have the same hope in our Savior. We all have the same claim to our Father's throne. We are all equal in our eternal opportunities.

The Holy Ghost is the bringer of this knowledge to our souls. For this reason, He is our peace. His peace is not as the world would present it; there will not always be ready answers, easy solutions, or swift trials with immediate eclipsing blessings (John 14:27).

His peace is not the absence of war, struggle, and conflict. The peace of the Spirit is the assurance of faith, hope, and charity, which overcomes the chaos of mortality. His peace is eternal, and it leads our hearts, minds, and weary souls to that endless realm where all things will become clear and all mysteries swept away.

Until that promised day, it is the Comforter we cling to with one hand and the Atonement that we reach out for with the other. The Spirit whispers to us with words that defy all mortal tongues, promising us with absolute certainty that in Jesus the Christ we are made whole, if we will but hold on our way.

The choice is ours, He declares; come unto Christ all ye that are heavy laden, in Him ye shall find your rest in the royal courts of your Eternal Father (Matthew 11:28).

The Children of God

As it is the divine calling of the Holy Ghost to make all things known unto the children of God the Father, so too it is the divine charge of the children of God to seek after all things pertaining to righteousness. Those of us who have heard His holy promptings—which He declares to us in our humble hours of scripture study and our lifetime of penitent prayers—share responsibility to bear our mortal witness, whenever and wherever opportunity arises.

This is no light responsibility. Therefore, the sacred task has not been placed upon our shoulders to carry alone. The remarkable kindness of the Gods knows no limits. While we are commissioned with the seemingly insurmountable challenge of building the kingdom of God on earth from mortal instruments, we have not been left to our own devices to establish such a holy kingdom. The Gods are with us. Or to be far more accurate, we are with the Gods in this holy purpose.

We are not left alone as we pursue Their works. The Holy Ghost, sent from our Father to bear witness of our Savior, labors side by side with us in this most sacred of callings, the declaration of the Atonement of Christ to all who will listen. He gives utterance to our testimonies. He provides words to convey the feelings of our hearts. He brings our thoughts into conversable clarity. He stands with us as we rise to declare the good word of God. We are not left alone, even for a moment, in our teachings and testifying.

The Spirit is with us, word for word, thought for thought, tear for tear, because our mission is His mission.

THE GODS I WORSHIP

This unity of divine aid is not singular to the Spirit. Jesus the Christ and God the Father are equally yoked to our personal wellbeing and our devoted efforts toward the welfare of all others. True doctrine, They teach us, is to love as They love, to give aid unceasingly, to never exhaust the well of our forgiveness, and to be ever mindful of those around us.

Without the confirming witness of the Holy Ghost, it would be baffling to ponder that with the unlimited powers of the Deities, we mortals—prone as we are to being frail, rebellious, and lackluster—are the eternal work and glory of the omnipotent Gods. Yet it is true.

That is their message to us and our message to all the world. All of Their powers, purposes, and perfections are fixed on our refinement unto exaltation and everlasting lives. We are not a side effect of evolution, a burden of an unwanted eternal duty, or simply a needed servant in a vast kingdom. We are the center, heart, and reason of Their holy beings. We are the children of God.

No mortal royal birthright, noble bloodline, or ancient inheritance of wealth can compare to the divinity that we all hold within ourselves. Each of us is a dual being: a divine immortal spirit clothed in the mortal flesh of the human body. This union of spirit and body constitutes the soul of man. While these two halves of the whole are destined to be separated by death, the separation will not be perpetual. We will be resurrected, our spirits forever forged together to live throughout immortality with our incorruptible bodies of flesh and bone, the same as our divine Father and Brother. It is in this state of resurrection that the soul of man is truly, finally redeemed.

However, our ultimate destination in His kingdom—the degree to which we excel, the boundaries to which we are corralled—is entirely of our own choosing. The Gods have made it possible for us to become joint-heirs with Them. This means that we too, in the process of time, can become gods capable of producing the same wonders as our divine parents have, and for the same reasons: the perfecting of our children.

Yet we can choose a different eternity, a lesser one. That is the wonder of our birthright as the children of God. We are agents to no one, not even the Gods. We choose our own path. We are not acted upon; we act. We are not compelled; we choose. In the end, while we are saved, sanctified, and redeemed by the grace of Christ's Atonement and not by a tally of our good works, we nevertheless decide whether we will allow the Atonement to have sway over us.

This does not mean that we set the pace, the course, the rewards, or the punishments of life, either in mortality or in eternity. The laws of exaltation are one eternal round, and they have been established and are governed by the Gods. There are rules that must be obeyed, ordinances that must be received, covenants that must be kept. However, our agency does allow us to choose, through our obedience or disobedience, which rewards we will receive.

Throughout the history of mankind, as recorded by the Holy Scriptures, the Gods have told us time and again that we will have our reward (Matthew 6:2–6). When this phrase is directed to the righteous, the idea of a reward is an inspiring, longed-for goal. When the same phrase is directed to the wicked, it conjures a chilling warning that causes us to rethink our impulses. This is the way of agency. The law does not change arbitrarily to favor one person over the next; rather, it is our approach to the law that creates outcomes as different from one another as earth's poles.

As the children of God, we have the power in us to decide how we will act. Although our circumstances are rarely in our control or anticipation, our choices and their established consequences are within our powers of decision. Once we understand that we hold this power as the children of God, and that this power cannot be stripped away from us, but only surrendered through the willful bondage of deliberate sin, then we begin to appreciate the magnitude of the life we are living now. The power to return to the Gods lies solely within our own will.

So how will we use this agency?

Will we strive to better understand ourselves in relation to the Gods? Will we take the time to test Them, to establish through our own experiences Their natures, characters, and purposes? Will we come to know Them? Will we choose to emulate Them? Will we trust Them? Will we love Them? Or will we use our powers of agency to reject the Gods who have created the universe for our well-being?

During the first estate, we chose, as we have always chosen, not in ignorance, blindness, or fear, but with knowledge, understanding, and power. We kept our first estate. We stood with the Father. We trusted the Son. We followed the Plan. Will we do so again? Will we hold fast in this, our second estate?

The Gods have not changed. Our faith in Them does not need to change either. Let us choose well. Let us choose the Gods and live as joint-heirs with Christ, clothed in immortality, eternal life, and exaltation.

But what of the billions who will not hear this message in this second estate? What of the billions who died in infancy? What of the people of past ages, kingdoms, empires, cultures, tribes, families, and individuals that perished without any opportunity to partake of an ordinance in mortality? Are they forgotten, rejected, or loved less? Of course not!

Such an idea of limited love and unfathomable unfairness flies in the face of all that the Gods have taught us of Their love, kindness, justice, mercy, perfection, and purposes. This is not the fate of our all-encompassing family. From the first days of Adam and Eve until the last days of the return of Christ Himself, not one human life will have been wasted or overlooked.

Every life, regardless of religious education or a complete lack thereof, will be given an equal opportunity to partake fully of the Atonement. In like turn, every life will be given the opportunity to fully reject the Atonement of Jesus Christ.

Life, every life, is blessed with equal responsibility to invoke our divine abilities of agency to choose the Gods. This perfection of opportunity for all mankind is found in the infinite nature of the Atonement of Christ and is manifested by the wonder of temple work.

Every mortal who ever came to this earthly realm will be given the opportunity to receive every required ordinance. Nothing will be denied to those who seek to unite themselves to the Gods.

THE CHILDREN OF GOD

Yes, there are some, perhaps many, who will not choose to accept this great work of salvation beyond the thin veil of mortality. However, make no mistake, all will be given the chance to make that decision. No man can be saved in ignorance (Doctrine and Covenants 131:6), and likewise no man will be damned in ignorance either.

We will all receive the education that is required to make a fully formed choice. We will all make our ultimate choice in complete fairness. No child of God will be cheated of his or her divine potential.

This is the gospel of good news! It is for everyone, not a select few. It is for all, the living and the dead, the infant and the ancient, the poor and the rich, the weak and the mighty, the enslaved and the free. Every race. Every ethnicity. Every nation. Every culture. Every religion. Every persuasion. Every human. We are all the children of God.

THE GODS I WORSHIP

Each of us, in our diverse circumstances, is known with the perfection of a loving Father that spans the eons, breaks the chains of death, frees us from the weight of sin, and makes all things equal in His unending perfection. He knows the very number of hairs upon our heads. He knows us. He loves us. He calls us home.

While we should strive all our mortal lives to bring this glorious gospel to all the world so that everyone may feel as much of His love in this life as possible, we need not despair at the daunting nature of such a task. The work of bringing the truth to every heart will go on in life and in death. This work will not fail, nor will God's purposes.

The miraculous work of spreading the gospel continues on both sides of the veil, for it is necessary for all to hear the truth. At this very moment, temple work is being done for the living and the dead across the globe.

THE CHILDREN OF GOD

In time, in order, and under the continued direction of the Gods, every child of God the Father will come to the inevitable opportunity of choosing his or her eternal side by accepting or rejecting the saving ordinances found in His temples.

Death is not the end of our hope. Life continues on, as does our spiritual education and responsibilities. We are the children of God no matter our nation, race, tongue, or religion. Whatever culture we were born into here does not eclipse our divine heritage. God is not cruel. His salvation is not limited. He does not have favorites. His work and glory are not to destroy and deny. He seeks to save us all, the spiritually educated and the spiritually illiterate alike.

Thus we see the beautiful perfection of a Father who has made it possible for all of His children to be joint-heirs with His Son, no matter the limitations of their mortal experience. Every circumstance has been taken into account, and all will be made fair in the everlasting Atonement of Christ.

We, the children of God, are all ultimately on equal footing. The Gods have absolute love for us—every single one of us. The only dividing line between our blessings and exaltations will be a self-inflicted one. It is not the Gods who lessen our divine inheritance; it is we alone who strip ourselves of all that we could have. That is our right as His children. We decide who we will become. We are in charge of our eternal destinies.

Our blessings, and our responsibilities, are beyond the comprehension of the mortal mind. It is easy to focus on the love, the reward, and the promised end, and these should be our focus in this life; however, let us not forget their terrifying opposites.

There are punishments affixed to sin. Once we have found the truth, once we have made a choice to stand with God, we can never again claim to be ignorant of that truth.

Yes, a full understanding will escape most of us. We will live in a state of faith, hope, and charity. Doubt will linger, sometimes loudly, at other times barely a shadow at our side. Few will have a knowledge that pierces the veil, although such a testimony is possible in this life. Yet no matter how slight our faith, how thin the stream of light we behold, we have nevertheless chosen a side and can never again be neutral thereafter.

For those of us who have made covenants, we are beholden to the truths we have been privileged to receive in this lifetime. We are bound by the promises we have made to the Divine. This does not make us better than those who will not receive such truths in this life. This makes us accountable for what we know and how we act.

To have a testimony of Christ is a blessing and a sacred banner that cannot be lowered in the spiritual war we are all engaged in without committing an act of treachery. Salvation and exaltation are possible for all of God's children. Unfortunately, so too is damnation, if we choose to curse ourselves with such a fate.

The Atonement of Jesus the Christ will forgive us of our sins as often as we repent of them. Yet if we do not call upon that infinite miracle of salvation, if we in fact reject it and the Gods who have given us this gift of everlasting cleansing and anointing, then we will deny ourselves a place in our Father's kingdom. It is not He who keeps us from our homecoming. It is we who lock the door at our backs and walk away.

The Gods plead for all to come unto Christ, to be perfected in Him, return to our Father, and go no more out (Revelations 3:12). They are our family. They are our home. They are the Gods to whom we may unfailingly worship for all of time and eternity.

They will not fail, and we need not either. That is our sacred legacy as the Children of God. We have the power within ourselves to seek Them out and to be instructed through Their teachings that They have established in Their gospel, taught in Their church, and governed by Their priesthood. They need not be strangers to any of us.

The Gods are nearer than we think. They watch over us closer than we dare hope. They love us beyond our abilities to feel. They are Gods, yet They are our family too. They are not distant; They are divine, and through Their plans we too can become divine. We are created in Their image. When we turn to Them, we return to our true selves. The Gods are real, and so too is our inherent divinity.

NOTES

The Church of Jesus Christ of Latter-day Saints has four canonized scriptures: the Holy Bible (King James Version), Book of Mormon, Doctrine and Covenants, and the Pearl of Great Price. Additionally, the Church has published study tools for the scriptures, two of which are the Bible Dictionary (BD), and Guide to the Scriptures (GS). I used these texts to form the primary basis for the doctrinal summaries found throughout the body of *The Gods I Worship*.

The following citations are the key passages and definitions that I used. Many of the citations appear—in some portion or another—in multiple chapters and are often

NOTES

used for more than one principle or point of the doctrine. Therefore, in an attempt to avoid redundancy, I have listed the citations alphabetically under the subheadings of the book of scripture they are located in.

Lastly, as stated in the Preface of this work, "it was impossible to cite every thought of theology without listing the entirety of the scriptures." As such, I once again recommend to the reader that you take your studies beyond the summary provided herein and go directly to the holy scriptures.

Should you wish to pursue any additional questions about the gospel of Jesus Christ, please contact your local Mormon missionaries at: www.mormon.org.

THE GODS I WORSHIP

HOLY BIBLE (KJV)

1. 1 John 4:8-10
2. 1 John 4:16
3. 1 John 5:7
4. 2 Peter 1:16-18
5. Acts 17:28-29
6. Acts 2:38
7. Ephesians 3:8-11
8. Ephesians 4:18-19
9. Ephesians 6:11-17
10. Exodus 6:3
11. Exodus 40:12-13
12. Genesis 2:17
13. Genesis 3:15
14. Galatians 4:4-7
15. Galatians 5:22-23
16. Isaiah 9:6
17. Isaiah 14:12-14
18. Isaiah 35:10
19. Isaiah 51:11
20. Isaiah 53:1-11
21. Jeremiah 1:5
22. Job 19:26
23. Job 38:7
24. John 1:1-4
25. John 2:1
26. John 3:1-3
27. John 3:16-17
28. John 4:10
29. John 10:31-33
30. John 11:33-35
31. John 14:27
32. John 15:16
33. John 17:1-3
34. John 17:21-23
35. John 20:1-8
36. John 20:11-17
37. Jude 1:6
38. Jude 1:9
39. Luke 1:27-30
40. Luke 1:41-55
41. Luke 2:4-7
42. Luke 4:1-13
43. Luke 9:58
44. Luke 23:46
45. Luke 24:1-6
46. Mark 1:17-19
47. Mark 3:13-19
48. Mark 5:40-42
49. Mark 16:1-7
50. Matthew 1:18-25
51. Matthew 2:12-15
52. Matthew 2:19-21
53. Matthew 3:16-17
54. Matthew 5:48
55. Matthew 6:2-6
56. Matthew 6:9-13
57. Matthew 7:14
58. Matthew 11:28
59. Matthew 12:23-28
60. Matthew 16:19
61. Matthew 23:37
62. Matthew 27:29-31
63. Matthew 28:1-7
64. Numbers 23:19
65. Philippians 2:10-11
66. Revelation 3:12
67. Revelation 12:7-9
68. Romans 5:8-21
69. Romans 8:16-17

NOTES

BOOK OF MORMON

70.	1 Nephi 11:13-34	90.	Alma 34:32
71.	1 Nephi 17:45	91.	Alma 40:2-3
72.	2 Nephi 2:8	92.	Alma 40:20-21
73.	2 Nephi 2:11	93.	Alma 41:3-6
74.	2 Nephi 2:25-26	94.	Alma 42:4
75.	2 Nephi 17:14-16	95.	Alma 42:14-28
76.	2 Nephi 25:14	96.	Alma 42:24
77.	2 Nephi 31:18	97.	Enos 1:6
78.	3 Nephi 9:20	98.	Ether 3:19
79.	3 Nephi 11:7	99.	Ether 12:27
80.	3 Nephi 11:27	100.	Helaman 14:16
81.	3 Nephi 17:14-17	101.	Moroni 2:2-3
82.	3 Nephi 17:20-22	102.	Moroni 4:3
83.	3 Nephi 18:19-21	103.	Moroni 6:8
84.	Alma 7:10-13	104.	Moroni 7:22-23
85.	Alma 11:45	105.	Moroni 7:47-48
86.	Alma 12:16	106.	Moroni 9:20
87.	Alma 12:24	107.	Mosiah 2:22-24
88.	Alma 29:5	108.	Mosiah 3:5
89.	Alma 34:9-15	109.	Mosiah 3:13
		110.	Mosiah 3:19
		111.	Mosiah 5:15
		112.	Mosiah 15:20
		113.	Mosiah 15:20-21
		114.	Mosiah 16:6-8

DOCTRINE AND COVENANTS

115.	Section 1:4	135.	Section 93:38
116.	Section 1:31-33	136.	Section 98:3
117.	Section 6:21	137.	Section 105:12; 33
118.	Section 10:5	138.	Section 110:1
119.	Section 13:1	139.	Section 110:13-16
120.	Section 18:18	140.	Section 112:30-31
121.	Section 19:16-20	141.	Section 121:31
122.	Section 20:73-74	142.	Section 122:6-7
123.	Section 29:36-39	143.	Section 124:33-34
124.	Section 29:41	144.	Section 124:37-39
125.	Section 39:4	145.	Section 130:19
126.	Section 58:28	146.	Section 130:22-23
127.	Section 59:8	147.	Section 131:6
128.	Section 68:27	148.	Section 132:46
129.	Section 76:3-4	149.	Section 133:42-52
130.	Section 76:30-39	150.	Section 137:1-10
131.	Section 76:58-63	151.	Section 138:11-15
132.	Section 84:88	152.	Section 138:31-35
133.	Section 88:40-41	153.	Section 138:58-60
134.	Section 93:31		

NOTES

PEARL OF GREAT PRICE

154. Abraham 3:21-28
155. Abraham 4:1
156. Articles of Faith 1:1
157. Articles of faith 1:2
158. Joseph Smith History 1:17
159. Joseph Smith—History 1:72
160. Moses 1:39
161. Moses 3:17
162. Moses 4:6
163. Moses 4:10-12
164. Moses 4:22-25
165. Moses 4:29-31
166. Moses 5:4-12
167. Moses 7:53

STUDY GUIDES

168. "A dispensation of the gospel is a period of time in which the Lord has at least one authorized servant on the earth who bears the holy priesthood and the keys, and who has a divine commission to dispense the gospel to the inhabitants of the earth. When this occurs, the gospel is revealed anew so that people of that dispensation... There have been many gospel dispensations...The Bible suggests at least one dispensation identified with Adam,... Enoch,... Noah,... Abraham, Moses, and Jesus...The fulness of times is the final dispensation and began with the revelation of the gospel to Joseph Smith." Dispensations, BD.

169. "Possibly the best known use of El is in Elohim, a plural form signifying the 'almighty' or 'omnipotent,' a name applied to the Father." El, BD.

THE GODS I WORSHIP

170. "Faith is to hope for things which are not seen, but which are true, and must be centered in Jesus Christ in order to produce salvation. To have faith is to have confidence in something or someone." Faith, BD.

171. "The [Fall was the] process by which mankind became mortal on this earth. When Adam and Eve ate of the forbidden fruit, they became mortal, that is, subject to sin and death." Fall of Adam and Eve, GS.

172. "[Grace is the] divine means of help or strength, given through the bounteous mercy and love of Jesus Christ. It is through the grace of the Lord Jesus, made possible by His atoning sacrifice, that mankind will be raised in immortality... It is likewise through the grace of the Lord that individuals, through faith in the Atonement of Jesus Christ and repentance of their sins, receive strength and assistance to do good works..." Grace, BD.

173. "When one speaks of God, it is generally the Father who is referred to; that is, Elohim." God, BD.

174. "The personage known as Jehovah in Old Testament...is the Son, known as Jesus Christ, and who is also a God. Jesus works under the direction of the Father and is in complete harmony with Him...Many of the things that the scripture says were done by God were actually done by the Lord..." God, BD.

175. "Although God created all things and is the ruler of the universe, being omnipotent, omniscient, and omnipresent (through His Spirit), mankind has a special relationship to Him that differentiates man

NOTES

from all other created things: man is literally God's offspring, made in His image, whereas all other things are but the work of His hands." God, BD.

176. "We learn from the revelations that have been given that there are three separate persons in the Godhead: the Father, the Son, and the Holy Ghost." God, BD.

177. "The third member of the Godhead and a personage of Spirit, not possessing a body of flesh and bones. The Holy Ghost has been manifest in every dispensation of the gospel since the beginning, being first made known to Adam." Holy Ghost, BD.

178. "[Resurrection is the] condition of living forever in a resurrected state, not subject to physical death." Immortal, Immortality, GS.

179. "Jehovah is the premortal Jesus Christ and came to earth being born of Mary." Jehovah, BD.

180. "The Resurrection consists in the uniting of a spirit body with a body of flesh and bones, never again to be divided. The Resurrection shall come to all, because of Christ's victory over death." Resurrection, BD.

181. "[The act of sealing is to] make valid in heaven the ordinances performed by priesthood authority on earth. Ordinances are sealed when they receive the approval of the Holy Spirit of Promise, which is the Holy Ghost." Seal, Sealing, GS.

182. "At the beginning of the Millennial Era, Christ will return to the earth. This event will mark the end of the mortal probation of this earth. The

wicked will be removed from the earth and the righteous will be caught up in a cloud while the earth is cleansed." Second Coming of Jesus Christ, GS.

183. "[The Veil is] a God-given forgetfulness that blocks people's memories of the premortal existence." Veil, GS.

About the Author

Zena E. Manley is a Utah based artist and writer who is perpetually trying to escape the Wasatch Front for the dales and vales of northern England. A dyslexic that barely survived English courses in school, Manley now contentedly introduces herself as a writer.

www.ingramcontent.com/pod-product-compliance
Lightning Source LLC
Chambersburg PA
CBHW032135040426
42449CB00005B/247